KINGDOM VISION

KINGDOM VISION

DANIEL P. PARKER

XULON PRESS

Xulon Press
2301 Lucien Way #415
Maitland, FL 32751
407.339.4217
www.xulonpress.com

Paperback ISBN-13: 978-1-66283-752-4
Ebook ISBN-13: 978-1-66283-753-1

DEDICATION

THIS BOOK IS dedicated to the wonderful people God has blessed my life with and that have always loved, supported and believed in me: *My beautiful & faithful wife Tiffany, our two sons Zachary & Jackson, our daughter-in-law Maria and our precious grandson Brian...you all are my blessing and gift from God Almighty and I treasure our family. *My incredible Parents, Danny and Betty who dedicated their entire lives to their children and their success...I love you and appreciate everything you've given to me, sacrificed for me & instilled in me Mama & Daddy, I am the man I am today because I was fortunate enough to be your son. *To my two very driven sisters Emily and Suzy, we have always believed in each other, along with their children, my nephews and nieces whom I adore.

*To my Mentor & Pastor, Jerry Braziel for allowing God to use you to grant me an opportunity with a platform to grow from. *To our awesome Assistant Pastor Tim Hall & his wife Gladys for their love & devotion as well as *To the entire congregation of Christian Fellowship Church…the CFC Family's love & support made this book possible. Our Leadership Team and Volunteers played a vital role of bringing this book to existence and I thank each and everyone of you deeply for your trust in what the Lord has given me. *To All of my Fellow Pastors and Colleagues who have spoken into my life over the years and believed for God's Glory to pour out on our Ministry. *Then of course to The One Who makes All Things New and The One in Whom All Things are possible, my Lord & Savior Jesus Christ for saving me, calling me, empowering me, guiding me, helping me all along the way…I love You Lord.

TABLE OF CONTENTS

FOREWORD

ALL I CAN say, is buckle up! Pastor Daniel Parker is not only a Kingdom Man but he has developed a Keen Vision for the times and the season in which we live. The reality that we need to be a part of a greater kingdom and the urgency for a clear vision is the understatement of the year. This is why I love what Pastor Parker releases in this book. This is what the Kingdom of Heaven should look like and this is what you will see clearly in the upcoming chapters.

Somebody say, Speak Lord! I'm listening…

-Chance Walters
(Evangelist & Author/
Chance Walters Ministries-Greensboro, NC)

In a chaotic world of polarizing differences, the only thing that can really bring us together is an understanding of the Kingdom. Pastor Daniel Parker in his new book "Kingdom Vision" reveals kingdom keys that will push us beyond the walls that religion has built and open us up to experience all that God has for us. I'd recommend this incredible resource to anyone who wants to see God's Kingdom established in this world and in their own world!

-Israel Campbell (Pastor & Author/
Flourishing Church -Los Angeles CA)

"Kingdom Vision" is a powerful book written from a kingdom point of view. Daniel Parker is an excellent writer and breaks down the topic very nicely so that everyone can gain the wisdom and insight that is needed to understand and apply kingdom principles to their lives. If we follow these principles that Daniel Parker highlights, I believe that it will set many people free. Much of the church is in bondage when we should be living as heirs of the kingdom. We may be on the earth, but we are not of this world. God never intended for His church to walk in poverty, defeat, or confusion. He wants us to walk in the blessings of the kingdom. Make sure you pray before reading this book, because the revelation in it will change your life.

-Michael Bacon (Pastor & Author/
Glory Tabernacle International Ministries
-Youngsville, NC)

INTRODUCTION

I PRAY THAT THIS book is an absolute game changer for your life as a Follower of Christ! My hope is that you not only read it but take it in deeply and understand fully the revelatory truth from it. This entire book comes straight from the Word of God. The bible is chock full of accounts that tell of circumstances that happened to everyday people of that time and how they overcame with the power of God in their life. That dynamic has not changed…we serve the same God they did Who desires for us to walk in that very same power! The Christian Life is not meant to drag through but to thrive in! We have the promise of eternity on our lives and that in and of itself is certainly enough, yet the Lord has given us a life with such abundance that He wants us to experience and celebrate just like the joy of our salvation. He wants us to live a Kingdom Life. The lives we live as Born-Again Believers is the preparation for the life we shall live forever with the Lord AND there are benefits available to us even now as Children of

God. Benefits that we do not have to wait until we are in heaven to get. There is so much untapped potential for us to discover and hidden treasure for us to uncover here now as we live on this Earth. We just have to have a willingness for more. The desire for more revelation, to walk in the God-Given Gifts of the Spirit, to operate in Spiritual Authority and Anointing as well as seeing what has been unseen and praying with an incredible level of faith can seem to be classified as "Super Spiritual" or wanting to be a "High & Mighty Holy Roller" but there is nothing wrong with wanting to be Powerful and live in Peace. There's nothing wrong with being powerful. Powerful people are effective people. They make things happen and not just for themselves but for others too. Most times when we think of Powerful People we think of Billionaire Business Moguls, World Leaders, Famous Athletes and so on and God can certainly use anyone who fits that criteria but He specializes in making the ordinary extraordinary! God's Word proves time and time again that He can use anyone for His Glory and He still does today.

"KINGDOM VISION" is all about how you see the very things you face, how you envision the obstacles of life from the decisions you make and the direction you go in, to the perspective you have and whether or not you can receive at the level you should then also how you view the places where others are…their standpoints and where they're coming from. This book was written to push you beyond the walls that religion has built and open you up to the real, rich relationship Jesus Christ longs to have with you that takes you to an even higher level! I believe that we are in a time like no other. The times we live in now can be confusing, conflicting and extremely stressful…don't do it without the power you're supposed to have! This power comes from the One who died for you, chose you before the foundations of the earth, knew you before you were even formed in your mother's womb, loves you unconditionally and has plans to prosper you and bless you with hope and an incredible future! WE NEED JESUS!

My hope is that you pray before reading each Chapter or however much time you set aside for this book and ask the Lord to help clear your mind and heart of every unnecessary thought so that you completely and clearly receive what it is you are about to invest your time in. This is not just a "read through" but a tool that if focused on intently will give you the mindset of whom God has declared that you are and that is a Kingdom Citizen! God gave me these Teachings that serve as Chapters for this book over the last year in the form of Sermon Series that I've presented at our Church each week. This book has not only culminated from the messages we have preached over the last year but also from pastoring for 13 years in addition to leading Worship in those 13 + years which has resulted in writing original music.

When God unleashed and exposed me to "Kingdom Teaching," the floodgates of Heaven poured into my life and has emboldened me as a "Kingdom Preacher" to see God's Vision for my life, implement the vision both immediately and gradually at times but always systematically according to His Will and Timing. I used to struggle at times with what to do next...that is no longer a problem. I hear from God at a level now like never before in my life. I fail and make mistakes still but I have a Freedom knowing I'm in tune with the One who forgives and grants grace and mercy. And it is not for me to take advantage of that grace, making it a disgrace but to also not walk in constant defeat and denial of blessings just because I messed up along the way. Like Grace, "Kingdom Vision" is certainly not a pass to sin but instead a better reason not to give in to sin because we see a bigger picture on an even greater level. Our Spiritual Sense of Discernment is off the charts when you see Kingdom, think Kingdom and talk Kingdom. Jesus taught about The Kingdom more than any other subject.

Why would He spend so much time teaching on this subject if it wasn't the way we were supposed to live? The fact is He has called us to live this way because He wants the best life possible for us now and later and there is no better way to live than with "Kingdom Vision!"

I truly hope you enjoy this book and will share it with others and I pray that the Teachings from it bless your life so richly that you will walk in God's Power everyday of your life and beyond. May The Lord Bless and Keep You!

Chapter 1

SEEING WITH KINGDOM VISION

FIRST OFF, IN order to see with "Kingdom Vision," we must know how the Lord recognizes the Kingdom and that can be uncovered by how He refers to them in the Gospels...The Kingdom of God and The Kingdom of Heaven. Also, when it comes to our Kingdom Identity & Authority, the bible says "we are more than Overcomers," so let's hone in on both of those aspects before we go any further.

Several times in the Gospels Jesus Himself identifies the Kingdom as either the Kingdom of God or the Kingdom of Heaven...in fact, He teaches Parables about this more than any other subject so He is obviously trying to impart something absolutely vital to us as Believers. Now, you may ask "is the Kingdom of God and the Kingdom of Heaven the same place?" ...the

1

answer would simply be that yes, they will be eventually. You see the Kingdom of Heaven is the "Third Heaven" that the Apostle Paul mentions in **2 Corinthians 12:2**. This is where God sits on His throne with Jesus at His right hand just as Stephen, the first Christian Martyr, envisioned as He was full of the Holy Spirit and near death **(Acts 7:55)**. This is where Angels & Cheribum bow down and cry out *"Holy, Holy, Holy is the Lord God Almighty"* as The Aging Apostle John envisioned in **Revelation 4:8**. This is where the Tree of Life is that John also saw that he notated in **Revelation 22.** Because of this, I believe that this is where the Garden of Eden (aka: "Paradise") was relocated during the Resurrection of Jesus Christ because there were eyewitness accounts of not only Jesus coming back after dying on a cross but also other devout believers in God **(Matthew 27:53)** . You see when sin entered the Earth through Adam & Eve, the Garden of Eden was lost and fell beside Hades, Sheol, Eternal Hell. This explains why in the parable that Jesus taught concerning *the Rich Man & The Beggar* **(Luke 16:19-31)**, they could see each other but there was a "great gulf" between them that separated them and kept them apart. This would also explain why Jesus told the thief on the right before dying beside him on the cross that *"TODAY, you'll be with Me in Paradise…"* **(Luke 23:43)** because Jesus didn't ascend to Heaven when He died on the cross, instead He descended into the "belly of the earth" or the "lower parts of the earth"

(**Ephesians 4:9**). He even likened it unto when Jonah was in the belly of a huge whale for 3 days and we know that after 3 days Jesus was resurrected and would then fellowship with His Disciples for several weeks until He would ascend to Heaven in front of them (**Acts 1:9**).

The Kingdom of Heaven is where the hearts (spirits) and souls (minds) of dear Christians who have already passed on reside in the Presence of the Lord (**2 Corinthians 5:8**) as they await the Gathering of the Saints who are alive on Earth in an event that has become known as *The Rapture* of the Church! When this takes place, then their flesh & bone, their DNA, every molecule that ever formed their earthly body from the grave they were buried in or wherever their ashes were scattered, will be raised first (**1 Thessalonians 4:16**) and reunite with their eternal spirits & souls and reform into their eternal glorified bodies!

The Kingdom of Heaven is the place we dream of and gives us peace when we lose a loved one who knew Christ simply because it's where the Lord is. Just as we said earlier of how Paul described it as the "Third Heaven" then to better understand it, you'd need to know that the second heaven is called the "Stellar" Heaven which is outer space and the first heaven is the "Aerial" Heaven which holds they sky and it's clouds that we can look up and visibly see in the very earthly atmosphere that we currently live in now. So then if the Kingdom of Heaven is in the third Heaven where is the Kingdom of God?...the answer is ON EARTH NOW BEING ESTABLISHED by every blood-bought, born again Christian who truly says YES to Jesus Christ!

We establish and usher in the very attributes of God's Kingdom every time we declare His Word over our lives, every time we represent Him on this Earth because we are called to be *"Ambassadors"* (**2 Corinthians 5:20**) of Heaven on this Earth. When Jesus taught the very framework of Prayer, He even said "...on Earth as IT IS IN Heaven" (**Matthew 6:5-15 & Luke 11:1-13**).

In Eternity, the Kingdom of Heaven will come down and join the Kingdom of Earth. This is where Jesus' Eternal Throne will be as He will forever defeat Satan's Anti-Christ and dethrone him after his attempt to set up a mocked throne in Jerusalem during the latter part of the seven year tribulation upon earth that I biblically believe transpires after the Rapture of the Church and before the Millennial Reign of Christ and His Church back on Earth. Yet as of now, the Kingdom of God on Earth is being implemented and strengthened through the Power of God in His people.

So, with that said, we are to function NOW with the mindset of Heaven as we develop more and more in our Relationship with Christ. By doing that we must have a Vision for what that entails and looks like, and we can do so by studying every single Parable that Jesus taught on it. I plan to do that in an upcoming Series I'm about to embark on that will also serve as the title and first chapter of my second book that I plan to write in 2022 called **"A Kingdom Culture!"** But in addition to the breaking down of those Parables, there are keys to the Kingdom we must know that we'll dissect in this book coming up but also things we must know that pertains to our roles in Kingdom Citizenship.

When it comes to our role…our very identity in The Kingdom and the very authority that we have as Kingdom Citizens, it's important to realize that you cannot have "Kingdom Vision" if you don't know who you are in the Kingdom. Who are we? The Bible is loaded with different descriptive elements of who we are in Christ so here is a few: the *Elect of God* (**Matthew 24:31**), *fearfully and wonderfully made* (**Psalm 139:14**), *Citizens of Heaven* (**Philippians 3:20-21**), *joint heirs with Christ* (**Romans 8:17**) and although there are many others, the one I want to focus on is *"more than overcomers/conquerors…"* (**Romans 8:37**). We shout that to the rooftops and have so for years in church but what does it mean exactly? I mean the role of an Overcomer or Conqueror is pretty awesome because they overcome and conquer, right? They go into every battle, every opposition, every conflict knowing they're coming out on top because that's who they are and what they do. They win. That role in and of itself is so encouraging and gratifying. It would be like the boxer or MMA Fighter who retires undefeated after a long, illustrious career of going up against the toughest opponents from all over the world. But here's the thing…the bible doesn't just say we are Overcomers or Conquerors but that we are MORE THAN. Well, if Overcomers and Conquerors overcome and conqueror what could be more than that?... I believe the answer is OCCUPYING & even OWNING what we Overcome and Conquer. What is it that we are to Occupy? The answer is TERRITORY!

You see, in the Old Testament when God would send Israel into what would be the Promised Land, it wasn't for them to just win a battle here and there. Not only were they to win the battle but also rid the land of whatever evil element dwelled there before and totally claim a stake there, leave their mark on it, occupy that territory, and keep their place there so they could own it. The Promised Land was not vacant so they could easily arrive and start enjoying the land flowing with milk & honey, no not at all, it had evil inhabitants that worshiped satanic idols and even practiced child sacrifice as a form of worship. God had more than one reason for taking them there. It was not just to give them a home but to rid the land of what was there. So, in order for the Children of God to possess the blessing, they'd have to face conflicting opposition that stood in the way. Not only would they have to seize opportunities to conquer but they'd have to occupy what they overcame. Meaning: they didn't just have to win, they had to keep what they won. They had to sustain their Victory through the authority of ownership. God didn't just want them to get blessings, He wanted them to keep them. He desires for us to be blessed and stay blessed. Now, don't get me wrong, I'm not advocating greed or hoarding and certainly not to be stingy with blessings to the point we don't share or sew. I know when He fed them manna & quail it wasn't for them to save and store up because He wanted them to depend on Him every day. When I say keep a blessing, I mean being willing to face down demonic opposition by declaring through Prayer and by the Word of God WHO YOU ARE IN CHRIST and see the bigger picture. See and spot what is going on behind the scenes of every hard thing you face...the fact is you are taking territory from the enemy! Taking territory is difficult. But once you have, you keep it and can occupy it by realizing the authority you have as an Owner. The reason we can consider ourselves Owners is because again, the bible calls us "joint heirs with Christ." When I receive an inheritance, I am the new Owner of whatever my inheritance entailed. I didn't have to work for it or pay for it, I simply got it because of who I am and whose I am! Understanding this helps us to think this way. The bible says in **Proverbs 23:7** *"as a man thinks, so is he"* ...when you think it, you'll see it, speak it, walk in it and walk like it. You cannot have Kingdom Vision nor function or operate in "Kingdom Living" unless you think it.

The enemy and his legion of demonic agents launch attacks through the Spiritual Warfare of the Mind.

NEWS ALERT: "The devil is NOT in hell!" Despite popular depiction, you need to know that he is not a little red cartoon character with a pitchfork & pointy tail on a pack of canned ham. The Bible calls him the "prince of the power of the air" **(Ephesians 2:2)** and he has been stuck between the first and second heaven ever since he was kicked out of the third heaven **(Isaiah 14:12-17)**. He dwells in our aerial & stellar atmospheres. Although he has not been to hell, yet hell was made for him and is his eternal death sentence. As for now, he has not yet been to the place of eternal torment & suffering. But it awaits him, his demons, his soon to come false prophet and all those who choose him over Jesus Christ. So, he is now amidst our atmosphere above us. That is why he attacks your mind first…he's coming from above not below. He tempts the mind to activate the flesh in its desires. That can be opposed and overcome by a stronger heart for the Lord that activates your Spirit to override the flesh and keep it under subjection despite its desires. Therefore our Spirit has to be invested in more so than the flesh. Harmful Influences for the flesh have saturated our culture and are all around us and our iPhone & android phones make it even faster and easier to access and engage. This is why we now have to take our need for the things of God to an all time high. Higher than ever before in the history of man because like never before there are so many more distractions than there's ever been. So many things standing in the way of having a pure heart & mind, going to church, prayer time, reading time in God's Word…you name it, there's always a strong distraction for it. The enemy wants to use distractions and harmful influences to keep the Lost trapped and the Saved struggling. But the struggle is over when the Saved simply realize who they are in Christ and the Kingdom Vision they can have to seize opportunities, overcome adversities, occupy enemy territory, and OWN our Kingdom Inheritance. The enemy is only being allowed to dwell a little longer before the End where he will think he has won but will quickly be defeated then imprisoned for 1,000 years, freed long enough to tempt one more time before he is thrown into hell forever. For now, God literally uses him as a tool to tempt the Unsaved to make a better choice and test the Saved to strengthen their faith in adversity and reveal to them His Grace through failures & falls.

Kingdom Vision is the way to see the best in people and in our own selves as well as hidden potential and the Glory of God. It will impart to you how God wants to intricately use you for His Higher Purpose and cause you to explode with love, appreciation, wisdom, discernment, creativity, and passion! Are you ready to SEE this way? Let's pray:

"Lord Jesus, equip me with Kingdom Vision, the way You see so that I can realize my true purpose, identity, and authority that You have paved the way for me to walk in.

I want to see this way so I can be more like you Lord…in Your Name I pray…AMEN!"

Chapter 2

THE KINGDOM KEY OF THANKFULNESS

BEING THANKFUL IS a huge Key when it comes to the Kingdom of God, and it unlocks and unleashes bountiful blessings upon your life! When you have a Thankful heart and a Thankful Life that let's someone know how much you appreciate them then you have more Blessings coming your way! As a child and even as I became a young adult, both of my late Grandmothers loved to cook for me. I could not go to their house to visit without them both trying to shove a piece of homemade cake, pie, cornbread, or biscuit in my mouth. They knew how much I loved it and despite them getting older and not feeling their best, they both still would insist on making me something because they loved me and loved how much I loved their cooking. Don't you want to bless someone again when they show you how much they appreciate it? Guess what...the same is true with God. He wants to bless and loves to bless.

Thankfulness ENCOURAGES God's Presence. In fact, Thankfulness ignites the fire that powers Encouragement unto God therefore "The Power of Encouragement from Heartfelt Appreciation can cause the Love of God to fill a room and overwhelm you with the joy of His Presence!"

Thankfulness will push out all the pride that can decay a person's heart, it can literally break down the walls in your spirit that bitterness and resentment have built and when this happens then God has a clear pathway to your very heart that He can send that over-whelming joy to! You see when there are blockages in your physical heart, you're in trouble medically.

You may either need a stint or bypass surgery to clear the way. The same is true with your spiritual heart if there are blockages then you are in trouble because you're unable to receive the good resources you need for a healthy spiritual life. I don't want to block the blessing, I don't want to hinder or delay anything the Lord wants to fill me with. I must choose to be Thankful so that I repel all pride and bitterness that could creep in my life. Also think about this: God wants to use your Thankful Heart to not only break down pride in you but also any pride in others. What do I mean? A huge aspect to Kingdom Vision is realizing where other people are spiritually and where they aren't. Some people just don't realize the problem they have with pride that can come from all the drama and complaining their lives are filled with. Yet your discernment and your love for God and them could cause you to help them realize it by breaking down those walls and telling them how Thankful you are for what God has done through them for your life. You're not being fake or phony either…beforehand God will show you a gift they have, their potential or something they did that was praiseworthy and embolden you to tell them. Then suddenly, this bitter, complaining, dramatic, prideful person has a new purpose because perhaps no one has ever told them how God has used them. The walls immediately start breaking down and a way has been made for their heart to change for the better. Now because they've been shown Thankfulness, they themselves become more & more Thankful. You had a Kingdom Key, you used it and now they have it and the Kingdom Benefits are spreading!!

Now remember, the Lord doesn't just want you to get a blessing, He wants you to keep a blessing… sustain it. And again, a part of your Kingdom Vision and Mindset is that right of Ownership that comes from your Inheritance as joint heirs with Christ that we spoke of in the previous Chapter but when you inherit something, yes you are the new Owner, but you were given a gift from your Benefactor that they didn't have to give but they did out of love and so we show our gratitude by being THANKFUL! This genuine component strengthens our role as Beneficiary, meaning we continue to benefit from what we have inherited and now Own!

In **<u>Luke 17:11-19</u>**, Jesus encounters 10 men suffering from Leprosy. This was a terrible disease that not only resulted in a horrible outbreak upon their skin but attacked their immune system viciously and could be deadly in many cases. Those with the disease were treated as outcasts and had to live outside of a populated area so as to not infect others because it could be highly contagious. If they had to come into town then they had to announce themselves as "unclean" which was humiliating. No one wanted to be around them, no one certainly wanted to get close enough to touch them...until they met Jesus. They cried out for Jesus to have mercy on them, they had heard of His Healing Power and had the faith to know He could make them well and their lives could change for the better. Jesus just simply spoke and said for them to *"go show themselves to the Priest..."* which was part of Levitical Law if a person believed they had gotten better and were no longer showing nor having anymore symptoms of Leprosy then they were to go and be examined by a Priest and he had the authority to declare them "clean" and permissible to return to society. This was an invitation by Jesus for them walk in faith. As they walked to where Jesus told them, they were healed because they would have to be healed by the time they reached the Priest at the Synagogue in town otherwise he would not declare them "clean." As the men went on their way, they saw they were healed but only one turned around and went back to thank Jesus. This man was a Samaritan, a by-racial individual that was part Jewish and part Assyrian. Samaritans were looked down upon by Jews. They suffered the pain and scrutiny of racial prejudice. The other 9 men kept going so they could be declared permissible to return to a normal life while just one realized the Source of their Healing and delayed himself from being examined by a Priest because somewhere deep inside he knew the Ultimate High Priest had made him well! Perhaps the other 9 men were all Jews and felt entitled to this amazing breakthrough while the Samaritan was simply Thankful. This man opened himself up to learn even more about God than ever before. Jesus told the man to essentially keep walking in faith because he would need it on after this day as we all do.

Thankful Christians soar higher in life because they're not bogged down by the weight of being ungrateful. You see, if Thankfulness doesn't fill your heart, then ungratefulness will and with that comes an overload of anger, resentment and bitterness that can corrode your Christianity, pollute your mind and dilute your power and authority as a child of God. Please don't allow that to happen in your life! Be THANKFUL! Focus on reasons to Praise rather than reasons to complain. The Apostle Paul tells us in **Philippians 4:8** that *"whatever things are true, noble, just, pure, lovely and are of a good report and if there is any virtue and anything praise-worthy then to meditate on these things."* That sums up the focused mindset of a Kingdom Christian!

Now with all that said, it is also important to be Thankful unto the Lord no matter what the circumstance or what anyone says or thinks. Case in point: when King David brought back the Ark of the Covenant to Jerusalem after it had been stolen by the Philistines. He danced before the Lord overjoyed but to his wife Michal, looked undignified as a King and the bible says she despised him for it in her heart **(2 Samuel 6:16)**. She chastised her husband for his praise and he basically responded, *"that he would act even more undignified than that for his God."*

The Scripture goes on to say that she became barren meaning she was unable to have children for the rest of her life. She herself should've been Thankful that the Ark of the Covenant had returned safely. It represented the Presence of Almighty God and they had been without it.

Yet she was too focused on Political Prestige and appearance rather than being grateful. This would cost her big time. *"You can't despise the Blessings of God then expect to be Blessed by God."* She despised David's gift of praise, so she never experienced the gift of motherhood.

There's also a back story to this…earlier on, David had suffered tragedy while trying to transport the Ark.

First off, he had put the wrong men in charge of transporting it. Levitical Law stated that only designated, anointed Priests could <u>carry</u> it and the men he commissioned were not Priests. In addition to that, they didn't even carry it, they had an oxen pull it on a cart with wheels. When the cart hit a bump, the Ark began to shake and one of the men feared the Ark would fall so he immediately grabbed it then fell down and died. Here's the thing, I truly believe God wanted the Ark to shake to remind them they were not carrying it correctly. When the man tried to grab it; he was essentially trying to contain what God was trying to move. He paid for it with his life which not only grieved but also frustrated King David. He had lost a good loyal man while trying to do something for God but would soon realize it was all because of his own negligence in how he ordered the Presence of God to be carried. David realized it was not God being harsh but himself being hasty. He could have pulled away from God and had the bitter mindset that trying to serve God is just too difficult and demands too much but instead he learned a valuable lesson from his tragic mistake and remained Thankful to God to be chosen to carry His Presence and to be forgiven. David went through a stressful, heartbreaking ordeal to bring the Ark back and yet was still so Thankful that he danced and praised God despite his own wife's displeasure. David didn't allow anyone or any circumstance to take away his Thankfulness…will you?

Despite more sin and failures in his personal life going forward, God would still refer to him as his son and "*a man after His own heart.*" We may fail at perfection but we don't have to fail at being Thankful...it truly is a Kingdom Key!

Our Thankfulness for the Blessings of God, His Mercy, Grace & Forgiveness should never waiver or grow weary. We have SO MUCH to be Thankful for as Children of God! We must remain Thankful unto the Lord AND others and with that genuine, honest, pure, heartfelt appreciation and realize that the things that have been locked to us, we now have access to because we have the key!

Let us pray: "*Lord, may I wake up each day CHOOSING to be THANKFUL for ALL of the Blessings You have bestowed upon my life and may that Thankfulness shine in every area of my life as a witness for Your Kingdom... in Jesus' Name, Amen!*"

Chapter 3

THE KINGDOM KEY
OF HONORING

N OW WHEN WE speak of the element and
aspect of Honoring as a Kingdom Key, it cannot
be phony or fake in order to get something in return
nor is it kissing up to someone or stroking their ego
for self-gain, rather it is truly honoring someone with
a pure heart from a place of honor within yourself. In
other words, as Kingdom People, we honor because
we are honorable. This does not mean we allow ourselves to be trampled upon by dictatorship or treated
like a doormat for others but it does mean we honor
people, offices they hold, etc...from a place inside that
sets aside disagreements and still honors. I don't have
to totally agree or agree at all with someone in order
to honor them. There are U.S. Presidents that I agree
with and have not agreed with but would still stand and

honor them if they walked into the room. It's a part of who I am. We are also instructed in the Word of God to implement this practice. The Apostle Paul wrote in the book of **Romans** & **1 Timothy** to not only adhere to governing authorities and obey the law of the land but also pray for the leadership. Although we can never agree with every single thing someone stands for we can honor them even if they are not honorable, we are able to honor them because <u>we are</u> honorable.

It's even taught in Courtrooms when the Bailiff tells everyone to "please rise" ...even the Criminal found guilty who is awaiting to be sentenced must stand in honor of the Judge. He or She has to stand in honor of the one about to determine how long they go to jail. There's no democracy or choice when it comes to it... all must stand in honor of the esteemed office held by that individual serving as Judge.

Honor should be instilled at an early age when it comes to our Parents, Grandparents, Uncles & Aunts, Guardians, Teachers, Coaches & Pastors. The Bible tells us to *"honor our Mother & Father and our days shall be long"* **(<u>Exodus 20:12</u>).** This tells me there is a benefit to honor right from the start of life. The very first people you learn to honor are the people who raise you. Growing up, I was fortunate enough to have loving parents. They both worked hard to make sure me and my two younger sisters had what we needed and even what we wanted at times. When it came to my Dad as a disciplinarian, as I got older, I knew how far to NOT push him. No matter what, I would listen to him and even as a young adult would still receive his advice. Even though the world had changed so much, his wisdom still carried, and I honored it.

My Dad has never sent a text, he's never posted anything on Social Media and has never downloaded an app but it didn't matter…he is my Father, he has lived longer than me and has always known what was best for me…I honor him. At the time that I am now currently writing this very book you are reading, he is very sick. He needs my help more than ever and it is the love and honor I have for him that pushes me through the hard times. I honor my Mother too…she is such an incredible wife and Caregiver to our Daddy. I have watched her push herself beyond limits and find strength that she didn't even realize she had. Her perseverance during his sickness has been extraordinary. I truly honor my Parents, Danny & Betty for all that they instilled in me through their words but mostly…through the lives they've both lived.

I am so blessed also to have my Pastor, Jerry Braziel and his lovely wife Lillie be part of my Congregation. I too am a pastor of 13 years this year (2021). I trained up under my Pastor as his Assistant & Youth Minister after I was born again in 2004. I watched him preach his heart out week after week, love people, pray for the sick and honor God. He led a church of just 13 people that grew to be a Campus that was totally debt free when he was able to pass the torch onto me. God used him in a mighty way to tell me of the call on my life. I wasn't even a Christian when he shook my hand as I was leaving church one cold February morning in 2004 and he pulled me in close to him to say *"God has called you to Preach Son and I felt it strong this morning!"* I'll never forget those words. I went home and told my wife and it's all we thought about that entire week until the following Sunday. You see, I was going to church because I was starting to pull the pieces of my life together. Heartbreak infused with alcoholism for over a decade had robbed me of so much. My wife and I had gotten back together after 9 long years of being apart. We had our firstborn son Zachary earlier on and never married. The Lord miraculously brought us back together when Zach was just 9 years old and then we married and had our second son Jackson. I had my family back and was now in Church but not in Christ. I had been avoiding altar calls for Salvation for several weeks in a row always anxiously waiting for the Service to be over and head towards the door overwhelmed with conviction. Yet the very next Sunday, I could not take the conviction anymore. When the Altar Call was given that time, I got up and went to that tear-stained altar and gave my life to Jesus Christ! My Pastor embraced me, my family rallied around me and this incredible journey began. God used Pastor Jerry to grant me a platform to articulate the

Word of God from and develop the craft of Preaching the Gospel. To this day, I can still go to him to confide in and get advice. Each year we still recognize and have a celebration for him and his wife and we reflect back on what God did through them that gave us the Ministry we have today. To set aside a day for the Former Pastor is unheard of in the world of denominations. My Pastor always urged that our church be an independent church led by God through the Pastor and Leaders appointed for that church. Honoring him is something we do first and foremost out of love, adoration and appreciation. But Kingdom Teaching and having a Kingdom Mindset and Vision also reminds me that Honoring him is a KEY!

If it's a Key, then what do keys do? …they unlock things, right? …simple, I know. So, if I honor him then there are things I undeniably access for me just simply through that love, adoration and appreciation I have that cause me to then use the Key of Honoring! He pastored the church I'm at now for 28 years! He preached thousands of sermons and led thousands to Christ. He ran a Ministry of Integrity with a high standard for that long. If I want to be successful, sustaining and continue to be able to withstand attacks and trials like he did then I must unlock and unleash that same blessing into my life by continually using the Kingdom Key of Honoring!

Honoring keeps you humble. Keeps you from every buying into your own fame or any prideful arrogance that could surface due to major accomplishments in your life. When I hit a milestone or accomplish a huge goal, I sit back in awe of the God I serve and the people He has blessed me with that helped me get there. Kingdom Vision allows you to see that. You're able to see such a bigger picture than your own self. You never have any need to ever honor yourself because if you are an honorable person who honors others then God will bring honor to you from others with blessings from above! To live and function this way is always a win, win situation…you can never go wrong with Honoring. If I am to be a long serving Pastor, then I honor my Pastor and other Pastors God has put in my life. If I am to be a loving Father and Husband then I honor my Dad and love my kids & wife the way he loved his and so on and so on. We must live lives of Honor!

Now with Kingdom Vision, you see deeper than ever before and because of this, you're able to see and discern weaknesses in others. You see their strengths and certainly focus on those but you can also see shortcomings which may result from a remnant of past hurts that cause them to fall short in a certain area or what not but here's the thing…you DO NOT allow it to cause you to see yourself above them in any way, shape or form…instead you HONOR THEM.

You honor their strength and by faith, speak life into their weaknesses by declaring the hidden potential they must make those weak areas stronger. By doing this, you have allowed God to use you to make someone *"sharper"* which is why the Bible tells us that *"iron sharpens iron"* **(Proverbs 27:17).** Plus, by honoring them, you have accessed similar strengths for your own life that have blessed their lives! What a great way to live, think and operate as a Christian! You bless and get blessed and stay blessed because you are blessed!

The Psalmist, Shepherd, Warrior-King & Worshiper David lived and operated this way.

When his brothers were lining up to see who the Prophet Samuel would anoint, Young David was honoring his Father by fulfilling his duties as a Shepherd protecting their herd of sheep from lions and bears and anything else that threatened their existence while at the same time singing praises unto His God that He honored daily. Honoring his own Father while at the same time honoring his Heavenly Father instilled a relationship with the Lord that absolutely stands out in the Old Testament. David brought so much honor to God that his life is still so famous for it to this day. Honoring his father Jesse through the tasks he gave him positioned him while honoring His Heavenly Father anointed him! Remember this "truth nugget": ***"Living a Life of Honor Never Leaves You Out!"*** This statement derives from how even though David was not in line that day when Samuel came to Jesse's house, God would not let the Prophet leave him out.

Samuel had approached every single one of Jesse's sons that were present and yet God hadn't called any of them to be the future King of Israel. God would not allow Samuel to just use who was there but caused him to probe into whether there were any more sons and there was…there was one that had been overlooked and underestimated by his own family but not by God. God always sees what others don't. That is why we don't have to be heard and seen by others every time…the most important one with more pull, influence, and authority than anyone else sees us. Young David gets called from a place where he was honoring to a place where God honored him right in front of people who didn't even think he was worthy enough to invite and include. "Stop worrying about whose attention you don't have, you have God's!" Later, after David would defeat a 9-foot Philistine Giant named Goliath, he would find a place of honor with Israel's first appointed King named Saul. With David by his side along with his son Jonathan, Saul's Military Might soared! They were unstoppable and all was well until one day upon returning from battle, Saul heard the maidens singing a chant that sung:

"Saul has killed thousands while David tens of thousands…" (**1 Samuel 18:7**). This immediately and drastically changed everything concerning the relationship of King Saul and David. Saul would right away begin

to despise David in his heart which would lead to him trying to kill him thereby putting David on the run. David would be hunted down by Saul and even have an opportunity to take Saul's life very easily but refused to due to honor. Others could not understand why he would not take advantage of an opportunity to destroy his enemy when they had seen him so bravely do so in the past with other adversaries. It was all because of the deep honor that resided within him that kept him from harming Saul. He responded that *"he would not bring harm to God's Anointed"* (**1 Samuel 24:6 & 26:9**). Saul would perish alongside of his son Jonathan on the battlefield against the Philistine Army. Saul would take his own life after seeing Jonathan fall, he did so because he knew the torment he would suffer. Someone else would lie and try to take the credit for killing Saul thinking it would grant them favor with David but because of David's honor for Saul, he had the man that claimed such a thing executed on the spot (**2 Samuel 1**). David did not play around when it came to Honor. Killing Saul looked so much like an advantage for David that in order for people to get a place of refuge with David, they naturally thought that having him think they took Saul out would be a positive thing with David but David didn't operate that way. He had Kingdom Vision that allowed him to see a much bigger picture. He knew he had to honor the one before him.

Whatever you Honor, you Access…whatever you Access, you Allow to enter your life.

What are you Honoring with your time and focus? Honoring is a Kingdom Key that will unlock and unleash favor, anointing and blessings on your life. Honor from a pure heart and honor wisely from a place of love and appreciation and you will walk in the favor of God for your life!

Pray: *"Lord, may I live a Life of Honor everyday & may You bless it as a Key…amen."*

Chapter 4

THE KINGDOM KEY OF FORGIVENESS

NOT ONLY DO I have the privileged honor of being the Pastor of CFC, but I also lead Worship with our band called FREEDOM. I love music, always have. I used to pretend in my room growing up that I was Joe Elliot of Def Leppard, Vince Neil from Motley Crue, Jon Bon Jovi, etc…all my Rock Heroes. I loved Country Music too…grew up listening to my Dad play Country and my Grandpa play Bluegrass. One of the early Rock Bands I was in before I gave my life to Christ was a band called Ruby Waxx and in it, I met a man named Clark Skinner. We hit it off and even roomed together for a while. We began to play a lot of songs just me & him with acoustic guitars. Later in years, Clark would have brain cancer and he did not survive it. I was able by the Grace of God, to lead him to Christ on his deathbed. It was one of the most surreal and genuine experiences of my life. Sometimes when I'm listening to online music while working out or something comes on my old radio in the garage while I'm working outside, if it's a song Clark & I used to play together I'll instantly think of him. Clark & I would play some unique songs together that we didn't play with the whole band. Songs like "One" from U2 and especially Don Henley's "Heart of the Matter." The Don Henley song has a line in it that says:

"And I'm thinking about forgiveness...forgiveness... even if, even if...you don't love me anymore." In this song the writer is essentially saying that he's focused on Forgiving someone who may no longer even love him. So, whether the relationship continues or not, he's focused on Forgiveness. What a great song! I love all the Eagles! Especially the Great Don Henley...and I miss my late friend Clark who if he were here and saw his name mentioned in this book, I know he would say "right on!"

That helps to set up the next Kingdom Key I want to discuss which is Forgiveness.

Forgiveness is more than words. It's deeper than accepting someone's apology. It is no longer holding against them the wrong they did, or you feel they did towards you. Forgiveness is releasing the weight of the burden that you carried from being hurt or wronged by someone.

Some things are certainly easier to forgive than others but nevertheless when we truly forgive we have relinquished a heavy load off of our lives and walked as Christ who forgave us of our sins. Jesus even said in **Matthew 6:14** *"For if you forgive other people when they sin against you, your heavenly father will also forgive you."* Like it or not, God expects us to forgive others.

So, if it's a Kingdom Key for me to forgive then to not forgive means I don't have a key.

Therefore, there are things that will be locked away that I won't have access to…Kingdom things…things of God…Heavenly Benefits…things that as a Christian, I wouldn't want to be without because quite frankly, I want all I can get when it comes to the things of God! I spent 28 years without walking in the fullness of the Lord, 28 years with no Kingdom Benefits then once I got saved, I then had to realize and learn about the fullness of the Lord and those Kingdom Benefits so in other words, I personally went without for too long when it comes to those aspects and so I don't want to do anything now to lock myself away from them so I must choose to forgive!

Forgiveness sets us free! Listen, the one you forgive doesn't even have to truly care whether or not you forgive them…I mean, it's certainly good if they do because it shows they're wanting to be better but when it comes to the wrongdoer in any circumstance, the greatest part of forgiveness that truly sets them free is to be forgiven by God Himself…that sets them free because there could be situations where the people they've wronged never forgive them but God still does. So forgiveness on the part of the one that has been wronged is how they get set free in the situation. God wants us to be released from it by doing what He does and that is to forgive.

So in essence, the main benefit to people forgiving is given to the one who needs to grant forgiveness…it truly sets them free and clears their heart from building up with bitterness, hatred and anger that can only pollute one's spirit and corrode their peace. There are way too many people walking around like that so please don't be one of them. This doesn't mean we allow people to do anything they want to us and get away with anything they want. You have the right to protect yourself, defend yourself, call the authorities, confront and even be upset…but in time, you must invoke the sweet release of forgiveness and simply let it go because when you don't then whatever wrong that was done to you just keeps being done over and over again spiritually, emotionally, and even mentally. People that refuse to forgive remain Victims instead of Victors. You are not a Victim. You cannot carry the "Victim Mentality" because it has absolutely NOTHING to do with KINGDOM LIVING! It doesn't mix, nor work so it's got to go in Jesus' Name! People who refuse to forgive most times are very spiritually immature people. They can be people who sit in church regularly but never grow in God's

Word so they never grow in Christ and live a Kingdom Life. Church is either a Social Setting to be around other people or it has become a workplace to clock in and serve or it's a "feel good moment" or something that makes someone else happy that they're trying to please but all in all, they're choosing to not get anything out of it because they're not allowing anything to sink in. They're not allowing their heart to change because they're not implementing anything they're being taught especially if that which they are not implementing is FORGIVENESS!

You may think that what you have been through is just too hard to let go or especially forgive. I absolutely understand that train of thought. Traumatic things happen to people.

Horrible things that they survived but a choice can be made to either keep living the nightmare or be free from it and the Key is Forgiveness! I have heard testimonies and even seen where people forgave the very one who murdered their loved one and had done so in court by the time they were sentenced. I have seen people forgive those who molested them or sexually abused them when they were children. These are certainly terrible, unimaginable things yet Forgiveness set the Victims Free and they are No Longer Slaves to what happened to them just as we as Christians are No Longer Slaves to sin because the Lord forgives us!

When Jesus taught The Lord's Prayer, in it He said: *"Forgive us our trespasses as we forgive those who trespass against us"* (**Matthew 6:9-13**). Forgiveness is so important and essential that it's included as a spiritual mandate when it comes to the very blueprint of prayer laid out by Jesus Himself. You cannot get around it or bypass it. In **Mark 11:25** He said: *"And when you stand praying, if you hold anything against anyone, FORGIVE THEM, so that your Father in Heaven may forgive you your sins."* When you look at this, the depth of what He has just said CANNOT be overlooked. First, He says "when you pray" so He's talking about the aspect of a Prayer Life which we must have as Christians. In this He realizes that we won't be able to pray with a pure heart if we hold the choice of refusing to forgive in our hearts. Second, He says, "Forgive Them, so that your Heavenly Father may forgive you your sins." "BOOM!"

There it is! That is a HUGE explanation to why Forgiveness is a Key…Forgiveness to others UNLOCKS Forgiveness to us! Just as there is NO Greater Love than the Love of God, there is NO Greater Forgiveness than the Forgiveness of God! It unlocks the door to Eternal Life and locks the door on eternal death. To walk in His Forgiveness is to walk in Spiritual FREEDOM but we are blocking that from us when we choose to not forgive! We can't live a Kingdom Life or have Kingdom Vision without Freedom and you can't walk in Freedom without the Key of Forgiveness.

Simon Peter once asked Jesus how many times he should forgive someone and threw out the number 7 and Jesus responded that he should forgive 7 x 70 times **(Matthew 18:21-22)** but Jesus was not stipulating that there is a "490 times" limitation on the amount of times you forgive someone...He was basically saying however many times it takes. Why would He stress that if it were not so vitally important? Set yourself free today and FORGIVE.

Pray: "Lord, may I forgive others as you have forgiven me, in Jesus' Name. Amen."

Chapter 5

THE KINGDOM
KEY OF GIVING

A LRIGHT, I KNOW what you're thinking already...another Prosperity Teaching from a Preacher about giving $$. Before I was saved and even after, my skin would crawl when I heard any Preacher talk about money. Gave me the creeps, rubbed me totally the wrong way. I guess growing up in the late 80's with the different scandals in Ministry that were plastered all over TV aided in my disdain too. Yet once I began to study the act of giving and sewing from God's Word along with the discernment from the Holy Spirit on who is legit and who may not be, I began to have a totally different view on the subject. In addition to that, since I've been enlightened by Kingdom Teaching, I have come to find that Giving is yet another Key!

Growing up I had heard people say that God only expects you to give what you're able to give which is true to a certain extent but what a person can do and what they actually do can be very different. What God expects is for us to be obedient and trust in Him. We learn in **Malachi 3:10** that we are to *"bring all the tithes into the storehouse"* (where we are fed so that there is provision) …the bible goes on to say in this portion of scripture: *"try me now in this, says the Lord of Hosts, if I will not open for you the windows of heaven and pour out for you such a blessing that there will not be room enough to receive it."* The tithe is 10% of your gross income. That is literally what "tithe" means…it means a tenth. So, a tenth is the minimum requirement in giving unto God. Offerings go above and beyond that. An offering is not a tithe neither is a donation or a financial gift. A tithe is out of obedience unto God.

Some would argue that the tithe should not come from your gross income but your net income instead because it is less money and a person cannot help that the government garnished their wages for taxes before they even received their paycheck. I absolutely hear that and thought that way too UNTIL I read my Bible. Jesus said to "give to Caesar (the government) what is Caesar's and give to God what is God's" **(Mark 12:17).** This statement shows not only Jesus' commitment to honor God in giving but to respect one's own country in the paying of taxes. Now when it comes to tithing from the Gross vs. the Net Income, think about it like this: The government (Caesar) takes the tax out first leaving you the Net. If you tithe only from the Net, you've allowed Caesar more honor and top priority over God. God has gotten a portion of your leftovers instead of your first fruits. The only way to counteract this in your life is to give by faith and trust in Him and tithe from your Gross Income.

Now once you become a Tither and it is a mainstay in your life, you'll see the benefits. You'll be able to look back and see how blessed your life is because of your obedience unto God. Since I've been a Christian and have tithed, I've not become a rich man but I certainly am a blessed one. I have more blessings than I can count and I lack for nothing. There are things I've yet to accomplish but I am still not lacking for anything. Tithing helped establish me as a Kingdom Giver which takes me to another level in addition to that. Giving offerings, sewing into good ground, blessing people's lives, etc… I wholeheartedly believe in the Mission Field and all that it entails. I also love to bless individuals with a lunch or some type of gift. I have given away things before that were sentimental and quite expensive but in that moment, I felt very pressed by the leading of the Holy Spirit to do so and so I wanted to obey God. All of these are great ways to sew into the Kingdom in addition to tithing. Even Churches as a whole should set aside their finances for Help Funds & Missions and honor those who bless the church in addition to the daily expenses it takes to run the Church regularly. How can a Church expect people to give if the Church itself doesn't give?

We started our own Missions Organization a few years ago to focus on not only a trip each year but local needs such as food, clothes, and God's Word out on the streets to those in need. I addition to this we also have Missions Partners that range from Literal Global Evangelism (feet on the ground), Ramp Building for Elderly & Handicap, a Recovery Campus for those who have recently been released from incarceration and the legendary St. Jude's Children's Hospital that specializes in fighting childhood cancer at no cost to the family. When our Congregation tithes, not only does it help with the operation of the church itself but the church sews into these Ministries that I've just mentioned. People at our church are also encouraged to give to these Organizations on their own, separate from their tithes.

Every time you give with a pure heart through obedient, biblical tithing along with sewing into trustworthy charitable organizations and even individuals that may actually need help or that you just want to bless, you are sewing into the Kingdom. You are building up the Kingdom of God which is God's System upon the earth. Jesus said in **Luke 6:38** to *"give and it shall be given to you."* He went on to say in that same scripture *"For with the same measure you use, it will be given back to* *you.*" So give in honor of God and with a genuine, true, sincere heart. Don't give so that you can brag about it. What you give should not attract a lot of attention anyway. You should do so discreetly always. Remember, your reward is in Heaven and it is from God not man. The bible even tells us that if we give to impress others then that is the only reward we'll receive. There is no reward from any source that can compare to God.

There is no form of provision higher than His. He cannot be out given, outsourced or out blessed.

There is no room in Kingdom Living for Greed in the form of holding back thereby trusting in ourselves as a Source. We are not a Source, He is. We are vessels depending on the resources that He, the Source, provides. He must be your Source. That is paramount in how you see when it comes to having Kingdom Vision. Remember that we do *"all things in Christ Who gives us strength"* **Philippians 4:13.** This means I trust in Him and not in my own provision. If it were not for the Lord, I would not be able to get out of bed every day and make a living for me and my family. He has not held back in how He has blessed me so how can I hold back in my giving unto Him?

When we give in His Name, we are unlocking Kingdom Benefits that simply come from trusting Him. When He sees how much you trust in Him, believe in Him, and rely on Him then He is moved to open Heaven's Windows and pour out those hard-to-contain blessings. Heaven responds to Earth therefore Earth activates Heaven. Everything in Heaven thrives, is whole and full of joy. I wish to walk in all of that now not just later when I get to Heaven, so I access all of this by Kingdom Keys and Giving is certainly one of them!

Finally, we know the concept of Seed, Time & Harvest. You may even be Market Savvy when it comes to Stocks & Investments. Kingdom Giving is Kingdom Investing.

But unlike the up and down Stock Market, the Kingdom is not something that fluctuates…instead it is stable and you never suffer a loss because of it. When you realize the instant worth of the Kingdom from the benefits you experience, you'll have no issue in sewing into it and allowing your life to be blessed with the access of yet another Kingdom Key!

Pray: "Lord, may I continue to obey you and trust in you by Giving and Investing in Your Kingdom…in Jesus' Holy Name! Amen!"

Chapter 6

THE KINGDOM KEY OF
PRAISE & WORSHIP

I LOVE MUSIC! MY family's tradition at Christmas time was to gather at my Grandparent's house and get out our acoustic instruments and have a jam session singing Bluegrass, Country & Gospel Music while all in a circle. Truly some of the best memories I have growing up was watching my Grandfather, the late Otha Parker (whom us grandkids called "Grandpap") play guitar. He played with finger picks and could play so fast and fluently. He was simply amazing to watch. His musical ability to play that way still astonishes me to this day. My Dad & I are Rhythm Players when it comes to guitar playing and my Grandpap was a harmony singer while my Dad & I are more Lead Singers. My Grandfather even played with some of the same people who played with the legendary Flatt & Scruggs and he was on local radio regularly. My Dad had the Country, Bluegrass & Gospel background but like every other 13 year old kid in 1963, his whole world changed musically when he saw the Beatles on The Ed Sullivan Show. He would be inspired by the Beatles and even be in his first band called "The Shamrocks" in the late 60's.

As a kid, I remembered having a 45 record of their single "You're Killing Me" and they sounded a lot like the Beatles. My Dad would go on to love the likes of Led Zeppelin, Creedence Clearwater Revival and even Rod Stewart but he would have a new awakening when he saw Waylon Jennings in concert. He'd then go on to be in several Country Bands throughout the 70's & 80's. Really good bands that would win local and regional talent contests with the grand prize eventually being a record contract for the band that wins it all. My Dad came very close to living his dream but would realize that his real dream was raising his 3 kids.

All of this played a part of my musical background. I grew up in the 1980's with the beginning of MTV. I loved all kinds of music from that era on up to 90's & early 2000's. I loved the upbeat rock sound and the over-the-top Power Ballad. I too was in some bands myself that covered a lot of the music that inspired me. Growing up in church, we strictly sang from the hymn books yet as I got older, churches were starting to put "Choruses" on overhead projectors and these Choruses were way more upbeat than the Hymns were. Artists like

Michael W. Smith and Amy Grant had been household names since the 80's and bands like Newsboys, Third Day & Jars of Clay had hit the scene of Contemporary Christian Music. All of these dynamics culminated in a church out of Australia called Hillsong that would literally change the world of "Church Music." The Legendary Worship Leader from that Church, Darlene Czech would belt out the classic "Shout to the Lord" and the rest is history.

There was certainly nothing wrong with the Timeless Hymns, but the Choruses took music in church up a notch and the excitement could not be contained. Praise & Worship Music was birthed out of those Choruses that had simply been added to most Traditional Church Formats. The meaning of the music had never changed but the messaging had. You see up to that point the songs were ABOUT GOD while Praise & Worship Music produced songs being sung TO GOD. A lot of the songs even sounded like Power Ballads from Arena Rock Giants like Journey which is fine because they wrote beautiful ballads. I mean, remaining respectful, why can't God have the Big Sound? He's so much bigger than what any other song has ever been written about anyway, right? I mean why can't His Music have state-of-the-art sound, technology, and ingenuity? When the songs are written, sung and played under the Anointing of the One Whom they are about, you simply cannot deny their impact.

I gave my life to Christ in late February of 2004 and had been back in church on and off a few months before that after the birth of our second son Jackson. Right as I am making positive changes in my life and getting back in church and on the verge of giving my life to Jesus Christ and on top of that answering the call of Ministry on my life, this dynamic change in Church Music is taking place worldwide. Little did I know how much of a huge part of my life and calling this would be. I would come to find in time that not only had God called me to preach and be a Pastor but He had also called me to be a Worship Leader. He had called me to break down Traditional Walls that had been built by Religion.

When I first began singing in church, I was asked by a beloved relative named Erma who was also the Choir Leader at that time. I had not even given my heart to Jesus yet but she sowed a seed in me by asking me to sing in front of the church due to my musical background.

At that time, I had also just finished out a 7-year stint in Radio and experienced so much in that field that helped me with my journey not only in music but Ministry as well. When I left radio, a big crossover hit was the debut release from Mercy Me called "I Can Only Imagine" and so this was the song that Erma asked me to sing because it was so popular around that time. I had a friend named Gerald Bunn, a brilliant & accomplished guitarist in our area, accompany me that day on the stage and I belted out that love song to Jesus. I felt something that day more than goose bumps…more than any adrenaline rush I had ever had on a Night Club Stage singing a Pearl Jam Cover. This was more…this was my Destiny…this was God. That was in October of 2003 and again in February of the very next year I was Saved! I appreciate and am eternally grateful for the invitation that Erma gave me and how my Pastor allowed me the opportunity to sing that day even though I had not yet confessed Jesus as my Lord & Savior. They both went beyond the walls of Religion and took a chance in sowing into the man that I would become instead of the man I was currently. That in and of itself is KINGDOM VISION personified! Seeing the future potential in a current state is how I would define Kingdom Vision. It's a big deal and it is essential to how we function as Kingdom Citizens.

After my conversion to Christianity, I immediately not only began to study the Word of God like crazy but I also joined the Church Choir and regularly sang Special Solo Songs which was a weekly feature in our Church Services at the time. This was a time where mainly only Southern Gospel and some Progressive Gospel music had been played. I had automatically started to lean more towards the Contemporary side and began to bring the music of not only more of Mercy Me but Third Day, Newsboys, Chris Tomlin and Casting Crowns. The Congregation seemed to really enjoy it.

After some time, my Pastor asked me to come on staff as a Youth Leader. I agreed and on Wednesday nights would start to play choruses of Contemporary Worship Songs for all the Youth. The kids really responded and we began to take them on trips across the states like our church had never done before but the experience and exposure was so worth it. We would go to Pastor Jentezen Franklin's Youth Conference in Georgia called "FORWARD" where we would hear from the biggest Praise & Worship Leaders in the world. We would also go to his church and see the magnitude of the operation Free Chapel was. This had a huge impact on me and the direction I would be led of God to take Ministry in when it came time, and my Pastor would pass the torch to me.

In time, I asked my Pastor if I could begin to implement some Praise & Worship Music in the Sunday Morning Services and he agreed. Now up to that point, I had sung these songs as Specials where everyone sat and listened. They only stood for the Hymns & Choruses when the Choir was on stage. This addition would prove to be a huge interruption to many. The Congregation had loved my preaching style and when I would play a special because at this point, I had been voted in as Assistant Pastor and had their support... until...I simply got on stage and asked them to please stand for the "Praise & Worship Segment." This was met with outright public resistance. The complaints began and yet my Pastor would say: "sing another one Brother Daniel!" Pastor Jerry felt the shift and knew the tide was turning. He knew what God wanted to do with that Church and knew I was the future leader God had chosen so the complaints did not matter because it was God's Will for the future of the Ministry there. I so admired his love, support, and courage under fire. Praise & Worship would ultimately affect how much support I would have as Senior Pastor when it came time with the current Congregation. I would face so much pressure and opposition mainly over music. Every single person that did not like Praise & Worship Music becoming a mainstay at the church still liked my preaching. For that reason, they would say things like: "you're a great preacher but not a pastor." The meaning behind statements like this, I would learn was because I didn't fall in line with what they preferred. It got even worse when I made the absurd decision to lose the suit and tie every single Sunday and wear blue jeans…this was a cultural shock for many. This proved to help me relate to even more people and new people coming in were instantly comfortable. I have nothing against suits, I have been blessed with several and still wear them on occasion but it is not my uniform. The Holy Ghost can move through me whether I'm suited up or in jeans and in high top sneakers. John the Baptist was never a dresser either and yet Jesus said he was the G.O.A.T. when it came to being a Prophet **(<u>Matthew 11:11</u>)**.

When I became Senior Pastor of CFC, the transition of music was still a heated issue and I wondered why...looking back now I realize exactly why...when it came to Praise & Worship, I was facing resistance because I was fighting for a key! Praise & Worship is a Kingdom Key!

Praise & Worship and the leading of it was originally the job of a beautiful, heavenly, angelic being named Lucifer. This job was so big that he fell in lust over his own hype and place of prominence that he forgot why and for Whom he was doing it for. Lucifer convinced 1/3 of Heaven's Army to side with him against God but they were all met with immediate removal from the Third Heaven **(Isaiah 14:12-17)**. Lucifer's fall from heaven due to his blatant rebellion turned him from a beautiful angel to a hideous creature named Satan that is stuck between the second and first heaven and amongst us in our very atmosphere **(Ephesians 2:2 & Job 1:7)**.

So music actually came out of Lucifer when he was an angelic being and it was all for God's Glory, not his own. When it comes to Praise & Worship, the fight has always been there because it started with him when he was in heaven serving God. Satan didn't want Praise & Worship instituted anywhere because he already knows how incredibly powerful it is. God removed him from that role and that entire territory so he fights against the move of it by causing resistance especially whenever it is initially established in a place of Worship. Satan had the key when he was formerly known as Lucifer. He knows the benefit to this key and what it can do for you as you serve the Lord. The release you experience, the favor that is poured out on your life, the freedom you feel…all because you're not ashamed to lift your voice and your hands and Praise & Worship the Lord. Satan blew it and cannot have it so he doesn't want anyone else to have it either…but too bad devil…God's people can have it!

People are even fought against when they're in church and they desire to Praise and they desire to Worship but they feel uncomfortable and shy…the enemy is fighting them hard because he doesn't want God praised and he doesn't want the one who is praising to have that Kingdom Key. Praise & Worship unto God has always been powerful and still is!

There was even a battle recorded in **2 Chronicles 20** where God had a King named Jehoshaphat put the Praise Singers on the front line in battle…not the trained archers, marksman, charioteers or swordsmen but Praise Singers. Their enemies were God's enemies so naturally He took care of them for them when they simply obeyed and Praised & Worshiped His Holy, Everlasting Name and He will do the same for you as well. Don't let anything, anyone or any feeling hold you back from giving your God the Praise & the Worship He so richly deserves…it is our gift to Him that blesses

Him more than anything and so it is the very key to his heart and what is Kingdom Living without the heart of God?

Again, the enemy does not want God to be praised neither does he want the potential praiser to access the powerful key of Praise & Worship. This is a spiritual battle over territory.

When you face resistance, most times it's because you're taking back territory from the enemy!

You look at the history of Israel and how they even originally acquired The Promised Land…God didn't send them into vacant territory but occupied territory. They had to not only go in and overcome the inhabitants and conquer the territory they had to then occupy it themselves and sustain it so they could own it! This is what being *"more than conquerors" is all about!*

So remember, Praise & Worship is not just something we do to open up a Church Service before the Sermon…it is a Gift for God and a Key for you and I… we must obtain it and use it! Pray: *"Lord, may I allow myself the freedom to Praise & Worship you so that I give you the blessing You long for and I reclaim spiritual territory for Your Kingdom & my life…in Jesus' Name! Amen."*

Chapter 7

Birthing A Miracle...

Now we know when it comes to Kingdom Vision, we long to walk in what we see.

Kingdom Living is believing God so fully and completely that you conduct your life with a Mindset that is all about beginning to live like Heaven on Earth. So, what I envision of God, I have in God. If there's anything hindering me from walking in the power of what God has shown me then I must pray for it to be revealed then see it removed so that I can Overcome, Occupy & Own the Territory where my Breakthrough Miracle resides. For me to walk and operate in Blessing, I have to "birth" things in my life. The Birthing Process is the most rewarding in all of life. The bond that a mother has with her child is truly special but when we begin to compare & contrast the spiritual metaphors then we have something on another level as far Birthing Your Miracle. Though the birthing process can be uncomfortable all along and horribly painful at the end, the reward is huge. Once a mother hears her baby cry and can look in his or her new eyes for the first time, all the thriving pain she just experienced seconds ago for so many hours all just became worth it. I saw it firsthand very clearly when my second son Jackson was born…the agonizing pain in my wife's face went to instant tears of Joy when she saw him.

Kingdom Vision from God is a Spiritual Blessing that must come to pass by God birthing it out of you over time. He does it by rewarding your faithfulness and diligence so that you begin to live out what you've dreamed and envisioned through the Lord giving it to you…meaning basically that you're now living in what you saw years earlier. Once you let God teach you through His Holy Spirit to see, think and reason this way then you'll apply it to every facet of your life. Kingdom Vision shows me the success of my family's future, the success of our church's future in Ministry, etc… you must see where you long to be!

So, in a sense we are Birthing our own Blessings through behavioral maturity, spiritual development, bold faith, biblical commitment, and all with a Servant's heart. It's a lot of different dynamics and that's why it requires a process and Birthing is certainly the ultimate process. Jesus went through the painful, passionate process of the cross for our ultimate blessing which is eternal life so we can endure a process to see the Visions He's shown us come to pass.

There were several "Miracle Births" in the bible before Jesus from Samuel & Samson, born of barren mothers to John the Baptist just before Him born of a woman well past child bearing age. What makes Jesus' Birth even more miraculous is that it was Divine. Meaning His was of a pure Virgin Birth. That's never ever been recorded as happening upon this earth except for in the Bible when it talks only about the birth of Jesus Christ our Lord. For young Mary to accept such a call on her life and to endure the gossip, assumptions and inuendoes, she'd have to have something to rely on and she did, she was visited supernaturally by Angels to tell her she'd supernaturally be visited by the Holy Spirit that would plant the seed for her womb that would result in the birth of the Messiah. "The unheard of" was as hard to walk in then as it is now, perhaps even harder yet Mary did. We too have even more to cause us to persevere and birth our miracle...we have the Word of God...we have the powerful things we have already witnessed, heard, experienced, and even envisioned. We can go through the labor pains in order to birth our miracle. God can unleash it on your life but He will prepare you for it and He will do so through the process of Birthing. So, allow Him to develop you wherever you need growth and watch how you're being able to eventually live in and walk in what He has shown you!

Pray: *"Lord, let my pain & intensity at times show me I'm birthing my miracle...in Your Name I pray...Amen."*

Chapter 8

HAVING A KINGDOM PERSPECTIVE

T HE VERY MEANING of the word "Perspective" is "point of view." It's how you understand, regard, and interpret. How you form your opinions and where you stand on issues. Perspective is the level that we learn at. When Perspective is enlightened then it is encouraged by elevation and a broadness that welcomes in all kinds of experiences and knowledge with all kinds of influence.

Our Perspectives are always challenged by division. Politics, Race & Religion want to control how you think. While I prefer a knowledge of the Love that God has for me in His Word through a personal relationship with Jesus Christ that empowers me to think higher, reason fairly, approach without anger, repel hatred, plan responsibly, work systematically, believe deeply, hear clearly and see supernaturally! When I live, think, see, operate, and reason this way then I have a Kingdom Perspective because I have chosen to see God's point of view first.

Now a huge aspect to having a Kingdom Perspective is clearly seeing where people are and where they aren't. Understanding where people are coming from and even having to see past how they may have approached you wrongly about an issue or what have you but the bottom line is seeing higher than anything determined to cause division. It's not about being the "bigger or better person," but being empowered by God to live and function at such a level that you avoid issues that may would've used to have been one simply because you now see it differently due to the Kingdom Perspective you now have. This helps us pray for people rather than tear them down or despise them. We are able to respond to adversity with a "take-charge kinda love" where people can't help but react but in a positive way and perhaps seeds can be sown to minister to them in how to deal with problems because of what they've encountered with you. Kingdom Perspective truly helps you tremendously handle people better. Especially those that you may engage with, but problems arise and you work through them despite moments of negativity, your patience and higher perspective get you through without escalation.

When it comes to forming Perspective, it normally comes from Experience but God would have us to form ours through the experiences that we allow Him to guide us through.

God leads and teaches us through His Holy Spirit. We are always learning from Him therefore Perspective is something that is always expanding. Especially when it comes to other people, He helps us to see where they are coming from whether it's right or wrong and grants us patience and focus on how to bring peace to the situation should it call for it. Realizing the Perspective of others, seeing from their viewpoint even when you understand but still don't agree breaks down barriers and helps solve so many issues in relationships giving negativity no foothold whatsoever.

If we want a Kingdom Perspective, then we must learn from the highest example possible and that is Jesus Himself. His Perspective ultimately IS THE Kingdom Perspective. In **<u>Ephesians 5:1</u>** Paul said to "imitate God" and Simon Peter took it to a whole other level when he saw Him walk on water, so he stepped out and did the same **(<u>Matthew 14:22-33</u>).** Simon Peter walked on water because he saw that it was possible from Jesus' Perspective. Jesus walked in what He saw was possible so when Peter allowed himself to see what Jesus saw and he saw how Jesus walked on it then he began to walk on it too. Peter didn't just see what Jesus was doing, but for a moment he saw what He saw and was able to do what He did. He would later lead the charge in preaching the Gospel because he knew Christ's

Perspective and he'd endure his own cross for the cause of Christ because from his Perspective he knew it was worth it! With the right Perspective, Simon Peter did the impossible like Jesus. Evidence builds Courage and Simon Peter was courageous and had all the evidence he needed in Jesus' example. But remember back when Simon Peter walked on the water, when he got his eyes on everything but Jesus, he began to sink. He fixed his eyes on the opposing, contradicting Perspective which was the wind and waves all around him which caused him to sink. Right Perspective allows us to rise above while Wrong Perspective causes us to sink...I want to continue to rise, don't you? So, I must keep my focus on Christ in order to gain His Perspective.

The Prophet Elisha had Kingdom Perspective in that he could see what God saw. He was a double-portioned anointed Prophet whom the great Elijah before him had passed the torch to and there's no greater example of Elisha's Kingdom Perspective than in **2 Kings 16:8-23** where he and his young servant are surrounded by an enemy army and his servant is frightened, but Elisha is at total peace due to his Perspective. He then prays and asks the Lord to let his servant see what he sees and then his servant can see above the approaching enemy army to see a vast angelic army of chariots from Heaven that have the enemy totally outnumbered and surrounded. Kingdom Perspective is knowing that there's so much more for you than there ever is against you.

King David had Kingdom Perspective too and he ironically showed it after one of his biggest falls. After he commits adultery with another man's wife, and she becomes pregnant and he has her husband killed in battle when he realizes he can't hide the affair or the fact that she is pregnant, he then marries the widow, and nothing is ever said about the affair but the baby dies just as Nathan the Prophet had said when he confronted David for his sin and David repented. When David is asked why he is no longer fasting after the baby's death, he replies "I cannot bring the child back to me but I can one day go and be with the child" …that is Kingdom Perspective. `David knew there was a better day coming. He knew the child was with God and that one day he too would be with God therefore he would one day be with the child. What better way to deal with current grief and loss than with Kingdom Perspective. It brings peace of mind and clarity to you. Yes, we still mourn but we don't give up or die in it ourselves. We learn to move on and move forward because we know all is not lost. Because we serve an Above & Beyond God, we must learn to live above & beyond what we endure. Loss hurts and we suffer but we rise above it because of who we are and whose we are.

Also, David didn't wallow in his own guilt either. The child's death was a direct result of David's sin. This was on him yet after he sorrowfully apologized, lamented before God in sackcloth & ashes, fasted and prayed and repented for what he'd done…he moved on. He dwelled on who forgave him, who now held the child and who would give him life in eternity so that he could reunite with the child…so God used Kingdom Perspective to help heal David from a devastating tragedy. David may have committed it, but he wasn't committed to it…he proved to be committed to God ultimately so no matter what you have done or fallen into just come back to the Lord again. Stay plugged into His Word, His Way, His Worship, and you'll develop this Kingdom Perspective that helps you see how He sees, and it will bring you peace and comfort throughout your life. With Kingdom Vision comes Perspective and it's a true benefit that must be utilized in our Christian Walk. Pray: *"Lord God, I desire that my Total Perspective is a Kingdom Perspective so I think, consider, reason, react, respond, operate, and strategize all on a higher level to fulfill Your Will for my life as a Citizen of Heaven on Earth" …in Jesus' Name…Amen."*

Chapter 9

SPIRITUAL TRIGGERS

NOW WHEN IT comes to having a Kingdom Vision, we must be firing on all the right cylinders and one way to do that is by understanding our Spiritual Triggers. They can be good or bad but they set things in motion either way. What Triggers you and what kind of Triggers are you activating?

Triggers cause Domino Effects or Fallouts to occur in our lives where things can either be spiraling out of control towards destruction or momentum has been triggered in such a way that growth and success are certainly firing on all cylinders so to speak it seems. The type of Domino Effect you trigger depends on the trajectory meaning it can fall into or out of place.

For example, look at the life of David in the Bible. I refer to his life a lot because he lived one of the most fascinating lives in all the bible and had an incredible relationship with God no matter what. His life was full of Spiritual Triggers. You see the Anointing of David by God triggered his battle with Goliath, his battle with Goliath triggered his battle with Saul but his love for God triggered him securing the kingdom. That's a whole lot said about one man's life in a nutshell but it's all true according to the Bible. When David was anointed by Samuel in front of his father Jesse and the rest of his brothers, he knew something about himself despite everything else…. he knew that one day he'd be King. He saw himself as more because he was and so are we! God has anointed us all for higher and greater things. So naturally when he brought food to his brothers' platoon and heard a nine-foot pagan giant blaspheming his God, Who had anointed him as King, he naturally reacted. His fame from defeating Goliath catapulted him to success as Saul's right hand warrior which in turn overshadowed any accomplishments by the current king which put David at odds with Saul but his worship and prayer life gave him a heart after God's own heart and he is loved, acknowledged and cherished by God to this very day because of it. His worship was a Trigger he could control and he did so in a fervent and powerful way. He could not help his fame rising after defeating Goliath, he just knew he was not going to allow anyone to blaspheme his God that way. He could not help the songs that young maidens sang about him that made Saul angry and jealous either. All he could control is how he responded. There will be Triggers in life that propel you towards prosperity and peace and others that launch you into turmoil, but God can use every direction, every trajectory for your development.

Jealousy and hatred are horrible Triggers. They have triggered so many terrible things throughout time. Adolf Hitler's hatred for the precious Jewish people resulted in the Holocaust which is still such a dreadful reminder of hatred in history. It's believed by many Theologians and Scholars that Hitler's lineage can be traced back to a man in the Bible named Haman from the book of **Esther.** He too despised the Jewish people and wanted genocide carried out on them. He convinced the Persian King Xerxes that this was best all due to his hatred of a certain Jewish man named Mordechai. Mordechai was a devout Hebrew who only bowed down to God and when Haman was being honored with a parade once, Mordechai did not bow. This was what Haman perceived as an act of dishonor and it triggered his hatred. Haman wanted Mordechai and all of his people to perish. The Jews were headed for total annihilation until Mordechai's niece Hadassah, aka Esther, took a bold stand. You see she had been picked to be Persia's Queen, yet she herself was a Jew. Her courage and love for her people caused her to speak up and expose Haman's hatred and when she did, he was destroyed and the death sentence on the Jews was lifted. Triggers firing for all kinds of reasons in this story but the bold stand for God was the determining factor and still is and always will be. With that said, sometimes you have to pull major Triggers in life that you know will shake things up but if it's your God-Called Destiny then you must.

Case-in-point…Jesus knew at the time He raised Lazarus from the dead in front of so many witnesses who would go back and tell the Religious Leaders (who hated him and wanted Him dead), that He was pretty much sealing His fate. He knew this would rouse them up even more and cause them to do whatever it took to have Him killed…He was right. The raising of his friend Lazarus was a Trigger that thrusted Him right to the Cross…but He raised Him up anyway because He loved him and wanted to give God the Glory! Like Jesus, we have to be willing to pull the right Triggers no matter the fallout, no matter who may not agree.

In the Gospel Accounts found in **Mark 10:17-31 & Luke 18:18-30**, we see that an unwillingness to believe that the Lord would provide his every need Triggered a Rich Young Ruler to go from excitement to sadness as he walked away from an opportunity to be a future Apostle. He chose to stay where he was rather than allow the Trigger of Faith to be pulled and join the Greatest Team of People to ever walk the face of the earth and change it for God's Glory. His unwillingness caused all of that while in **Luke 8:43-48** we see the opposite in a woman with a 12 year long uncontrollable bleeding issue. She is willing to fight through a crowd and push her way in despite being so sick and weak because she has faith to know if she can just touch the very hem of His garment, she'll be made whole. The Rich Young Ruler is Unwilling to pull the Trigger of Willingness while the Woman has no issue whatsoever and she also never has another blood issue again either. What Triggers you...willingness or unwillingness? ... belief or unbelief? ...hope or doubt? ...faith or sight? ...what is your Trigger?

Finally, the Ultimate Spiritual Trigger is the one that will set in motion the end of the world as we now know it and begin what is called The Great Tribulation and that Trigger is called The Rapture.

When the Rapture of Jesus' Church takes place, the Born-Again Christian's Kingdom Vision will be perfected with the transformation of their new glorified body. While those left behind on earth who may have had some bible knowledge will begin to develop the Kingdom Vision and knowledge they'll need to possibly survive the next horrible 7 years or develop the peace and courage they'll need to take a stand and be martyred for what they finally passionately believe. This Ultimate Trigger ushers in the most crooked, corrupt government ever that will be led by the Anti-Christ who is believed to come from the Middle East while his forerunner the False Prophet it is believed will be head of one of the most powerful and influential Christian Denominations. Although the Rapture Triggers the

Great Tribulation on earth, the Great Tribulation Triggers the Millennial Reign! This is when WE return with Jesus for His Second Coming and the Anti-Christ and False Prophet are arrested and chained for 1,000 years. We reign with Christ on Earth as it is being made new and awaiting to join with Heaven as it comes down and forms The New Jerusalem! At the end of 1,000 years, Satan is released one last time to tempt those born Post Rapture so they too will have the choice to choose between good and evil. Once their decision is made Satan and all those who choose him will be cast into the Lake of Fire (hell) forever while we who choose Jesus will enjoy Eternity in the New Heaven & Earth where our Kingdom Vision is totally and completely perfected!

While an absolute knowledge of all End Times Events is not possible, having some knowledge is very helpful in implementing Kingdom Vision. The late Dr. Jack Van Impe wrote an outstanding book called "REVELATION REVEALED" that I highly recommend when it comes to End Times. He wrote it "expository-style" so every Chapter & Verse of the book of Revelation is explained in radiant detail. I too have available an extensive cd set of teachings where we had an expository teaching from the book of Revelation for well over a year in order to dissect and learn more about this fascinating book from God's Word that promises a special blessing for reading it and knowing it. Pray:

"Lord, help me pull the right Spiritual Triggers in life and remain prepared for the Ultimate Trigger that is Your Rapture in You I pray, Amen"

Chapter 10

Doorways To Destiny

Now we are reaching the latter part of this book. After this Chapter, there will be one more following a Conclusion. This particular chapter is a favorite of mine because I love to discuss the aspect of Destiny and the great things we have in store as Children of God! It's important to realize that life is full of "doors" so to speak that can present opportunities or seasons that begin or end but also there are doors that come in the form of decisions that we are faced with and because it's a door, we either open it and walk through or let God open it and we walk through, or we could also close it or let God close it.

Now a very Super Spiritual Statement could be made right about now that would sound something like this: "we need to let God and only God open and close doors in our life" and yes, that is very Scriptural because we know that in **Revelation 3:8** that Jesus "opens doors that no man could close" but I do believe there are times when God expects us to shut doors.

We have free will and we must make decisions to act, not act, etc… I mean the Lord has always wanted to give me eternal life through salvation but I had to make the decision to answer the altar call and respond by changing my life and living for Him…amen? He was knocking at my heart's door through conviction but I had to open the door to let Him in.

So again, the "doors" in life can be opportunities or decisions, choices that we make.

The Doorways to our Destiny will come in the form of opportunities that open up a way for us to grow, develop and make Kingdom Connections that further strengthen our Kingdom Vision! It could be a volunteering venture at your local Church or a Community Outreach.

Of course, a new job or to embark on your Career Path are all awesome opportunities but also, things you never thought you'd do but you feel an incredible urge to do like what I'm doing right now: I NEVER IN A MILLION YEARS THOUGHT I'D WRITE A BOOK…lol. What kind of opportunities have or have the potential to present themselves to you? Will you take a chance and examine it to see if it's right for you or will you dismiss it? A lot of times, awesome opportunities can come our way, but we ignore it or put it off because it could require some work or intensified effort on our part. Don't be afraid of the work, don't be weary of further delving into it to see if it's God's will and His plan for your life. A Doorway to your Destiny is never a waste of time!

Decisions and Choices are also Doors. How you decide, how you choose controls what that Door does and how it affects your life. Some choices are low impact but some have a huge impact. What we decide, what we choose can open ourselves up to the things we need and unfortunately, the things we don't need.

When it comes to Doorways to our Destiny, it's about embracing the right opportunities and making the right decisions that all open the right doors and close the wrong ones so that we reach our full potential, fulfill our Kingdom Assignment, and walk in our own Spirit-Led Destiny!

I have also learned that we inadvertently at times, close doors that should've never been closed and we open doors that should've never been opened. It's time to shut what needs to be closed and revisit what needs to be opened. Most times we know these instances have come through the regret we feel and our 20/20 hindsight. Looking back on something we do in fact see clearer most times…so…let's use that to our advantage and do something with it.

Reality will say it's over and you can't go back or there's nothing that can be done now…that is nonsense when it comes to Kingdom Living! Kingdom Living is all about LIVING YOUR BEST LIFE NOW! So, in order to do that, we need to take advantage of ANY missed opportunities that we let pass by, by taking another look at them while also, making big moves to shut down anything that we now see we should've never gotten ourselves into. Yes, there will always be consequences from our actions to deal with but when it comes to Kingdom Living and having Kingdom Vision, we can't settle for being stuck. When you are stuck, you are miserable and unproductive. That's not Kingdom Living. We are called to be The Elect of God, The Bride and Church of Christ. We are to live at a higher level not a lofty level to boast from but a higher one that sees above all the chaos and confusion and the different petty things that trip people up but also the unbeliev-able things that befall upon our culture.

We are at a time right now where there seems to be something different each year to divide society from race to political elections to a pandemic and now a vac-cine. The spirit of division is everywhere you turn but what do we choose? My choice is to see with Kingdom Vision and to represent Christ in all of this. Do I get frustrated with Fake News? -absolutely. Do I get upset about our Country's direction? -you better believe it. Do I have an emboldened opinion about politics and government that has been enlightened and educated through the years from my time as a News Talk Radio Station Manager to my calling as a Senior Pastor of a

Church for over 13 years? -of course I do. Yet when it comes to all those divisive topics, I'm personally mindful of which doors I open and which ones I abruptly shut. We want to reach as many people for the cause of Christ as possible while at the same time not subjecting ourselves to the influences that are harming our society and culture. We are to reach the lost but our own hearts cannot be contaminated in the process. We can sit down with other believers who's take on political issues, etc... may be different than ours and have peace and certainly, some common ground without judging or questioning their Christianity or even more over the top like sending them to hell in our mind simply because we don't see eye to eye on things. I mean especially if we are dealing with people who love Jesus but they vote differently.

We have common ground...His Name is Jesus!

I choose to walk in Doors where I can have an opportunity to bring people together but at the same time still stand for what I believe so don't think for one minute that I advocate in any way, shape or form compromising or backing down depending on who you are with. No, I do not but I also believe in relating so I can reach. Paul said in **1 Corinthians 9:22** "I have become all things to all people so that by all means some might be saved." This did not mean he sold out or backed down it just simply meant that he went into the situation knowing who he was and knowing who they were.

That's living above the lowly things that divide. That's living higher than the chaos & confusion. That's living and seeing above and beyond all the petty things that make people fight and despise one another. I choose to open a better door and have a destiny that enjoys life, loves people, and lifts up the name of Jesus.

Our Destiny as Christians is to show people Jesus. How can I show people Jesus if I shut them down automatically just because there are things they say, think or stand for that I don't agree with? I don't get to reach only Conservatives for Christ…I must reach Liberals too. I must be willing and equipped to go into any environment for the cause of Christ…that is my Destiny.

Destiny will take you to uncomfortable places at times. Places you didn't quite envision at first but you realize that there's a purpose there bigger than you and that God is positioning you to make an impact. That's my goal in every opportunity that presents a door for me to walk in…I WANT TO MAKE AN IMPACT FOR HIS KINGDOM! I have an assignment from the Highest Office in all of Creation. We are all on assignment as Christians and Kingdom Citizens.

We have a duty to fulfill. When you agree to live this way, God will begin to open doors all over the place for you. He just needs willing vessels to obey Him!

You see with KINGDOM VISION comes a Kingdom Mentality in how to live each day with even greater purpose. When you wake up each day knowing who you are, Who you belong to, the enormity of what it is you are a part of, the magnitude of what you are an heir to and the incredible benefits you have access to…THEN…you truly can walk in courage, confidence, joy and *peace that certainly surpasses all understanding* (**Philippians 4:6**).

It's important to realize that Religion does not allow this. Religion will not allow this way of life or this way of thinking because of the constant reminders of failures. Religion will not allow this lifestyle because of the constant thoughts of you not measuring up or someone else or even some kind of situation not measuring up. Religion always leaves a void. It always leaves a deficit. Religion has you judging others and keeping score too much to ever focus in closely on Kingdom Living.

Another thing that will hinder your Kingdom Assignment and get your eyes away from Kingdom Vision and Destiny is Immaturity. Immaturity will always make everything about you and that's not how Kingdom Living works. Kingdom Living is ALL ABOUT HIM! Immaturity will always make you out to be the victim in most scenarios as well as intensify ANY amount of drama you may possibly have simply because Immaturity feeds on it. Immaturity lives off of drama and everything related to it. You'll never rise up if you don't grow up. That mindset has to go so that you can experience your amazing Kingdom Destiny. God has a Doorway for you but Religion & Immaturity must be left behind. I choose a Relationship with Christ over Religion. I choose to grow in Truth over wallowing in Immature Drama. I choose Jesus and His Kingdom Over everything else! This is the way we are called to live…let's live our best life now!

PRAY: "*Lord, help me to recognize the Doorways to Destiny that present themselves in my life so that I don't miss an opportunity to advance forward in the plan you have for me… in Jesus' Name, AMEN!*"

Chapter 11

VISIONS OF VICTORY

FINALLY, WHEN IT comes to having KINGDOM VISION, we must talk about the precedent that we put on the Victorious Visions that God grants us and how we should let them be a mainstay, so to speak, in our lives. It doesn't mean we ignore hard times or difficult subjects and situations but it does mean that we have refused to be sidetracked from our main focus as a Kingdom Christian and that is NO MATTER WHAT, WE ARE ON THE WINNING SIDE!

When you choose to wake up every day and KNOW that there is so much more for you than there ever could be against you then you'll approach each day of your life with a passion and excitement that truly shows the attributes of being more than an overcomer! This mindset and approach to life is not a fairy tale it's simply a better way to live. Too many Christians are suffering from the depths of depression. There is just too much despair and burdensome troubles in the lives of God's Elect People these days and there always has been. The Lord has and always has had a cure for this detrimental way of living and it's through VISIONS OF VICTORY!

The Lord knows your struggles and the things that weigh you down. He has been right there with you through it all. There's not a thing you've endured or imagined that has hurt you that He has not seen you go through. He loves you more than anyone else in your life so naturally He wants to help and give you what you need to not just cope but CONQUOR!

The enemy would love for you to dwell each day on your failures and amplify all hopelessness but the Lord can totally tear all that dreadfulness down in one fail swoop by empowering you with a Victorious Vision of you coming out on the other side of your trial and succeeding greatly in your life! You just got to want Him to show you and you got to want to see it!

This is not about wanting to see things that are not there or not real or that will never happen. NO...there is also with VISIONS OF VICTORY the absolute critical element of Faith! The Vision has to be from God not your flesh and when He reveals the Vision to you, you must believe it and trust by Faith then embrace it for your life and claim it to come to pass. You got to constantly see it and know it is coming like second nature. Meaning you don't doubt it coming to pass no more than believing something that has already happened in your life…it's that automatic. There's no denying it. It will happen!

Victorious Visions are what God uses to pull us through the hard times of life. He knows the suffering one can endure in life. He knows the hard times that we face. He has not left us with no remedy. God always has us moving forward, moving towards the goal. Kingdom Living is always about advancing forward and we can move forward despite any amount of grief through the power of Victorious Visions from God!

When I think about Joseph in the Bible, he had to have something powerful to make it through a decade or more of unfairness. He had to have something moving him forward despite all the mistreatment and agony, he had endured…the fact is he did…he had a real, tangible relationship with God…AND…he had a VISION OF VICTORY!

The Bible spends nearly 13 full chapters telling Joseph's story **(Genesis Chapters 37-50).**

It all begins with him having dreams…visions from God about himself ruling over his family in an esteemed place of authority & honor. Certainly, at the initial time of the vision, Joseph didn't know the fullness of what God was showing him. He began to describe it to his family and was scoffed for it. His parents were offended by it and his brothers despised him even more. You see they already despised him due to the favoritism from their Father Jacob. This vision from Joseph seemed pompous and boastful to them which is somewhat understandable but when you really think about it, it is kind of difficult not to come across the wrong way when you're explaining a vision of yourself reigning over the very ones you are explaining the vision to. Then he has yet another vision which is similar to the first, again he reigns and rules from a place of prominence. All this on top of the fact that their Father Jacob had given Joseph a beautiful coat of many colors was now just too much for his brothers to handle. Their jealousy for Joseph turned to hatred and it overwhelmed them to the point of making a rash decision. They decided to kill him until one of the brothers, Judah spoke up. Judah convinced the rest to not take their brother Joseph's life. They had thrown him into a pit for the time being then sold him to Slave Traders who then transported him to Egypt. The brothers took Joseph's coat of many colors and soaked it into the blood of a lamb they killed. They took the coat to their Father Jacob and lied to him claiming that the coat was all they had found of him and that wild animals must have torn him to pieces. Jacob mourned over Joseph from that day.

Joseph is immediately sold as soon as he arrives in Egypt to a reputable Leader named Potiphar who served in the Administration of the current Pharoah of that day. Joseph is a slave in Egypt but he has a Vision of Victory…he had not forgotten what God showed him. Soon, Potiphar can see the uniqueness of Joseph. He can tell that he is gifted. This was God's Favor and Anointing on Joseph's life…even a pagan unbeliever could see there was something incredibly special about this young man. Everything in Potiphar's household ran better with Joseph there to the point that Potiphar put Joseph over his entire house. So, Joseph was betrayed by his own brothers by being thrown in a pit and sold into slavery yet exceled…he advanced in it and moved forward. Remember, that is where KINGDOM VISION always takes you…advancing forward and continuing to rise no matter where you've fallen!

Joseph at this point has made the best of the situation but then temptation comes. It comes from Potiphar's wife who wants to have an affair with Joseph. She backs him into a corner but he refuses to sin against God and against Potiphar. She rips part of his garment off leaving him nearly naked. He runs out of the room, and she cries out that she's been raped by him. A blatant lie no doubt but the situation looks bad. Joseph is half naked and running away while she's crying with his clothes in her hand. Potiphar had no choice but to have him put in prison. Joseph goes from being betrayed by his brothers, sold into slavery now put in prison for a crime he did not commit. He had done the right thing by God and Potiphar but still was treated guilty because of a lie. All of this had to have weighed on him tremendously and could've made him give up but something kept him going…HE HAD A VISION OF VICTORY!

What may have seemed like it was Rock Bottom was really the verge of his breakthrough! You see, while in prison he interprets another inmate's dream. This is told all over the prison that Joseph has this spiritual ability. The day would come when the Pharoah himself would need to have a dream interpreted and Joseph's name is brought up. The Pharoah summons him to the palace and he interprets the Pharoah's dream. The interpretation of the dream consisted in 7 years of plenty followed by 7 years of famine. Because of this, the Pharoah makes Joseph the Governor under him over all of Egypt so he can coordinate the stockpile of resources saved up over the 7 years of plenty in order to survive the coming famine.

When the famine hit, neighboring regions would come to Egypt from all over to get resources. Joseph's own brothers would come. They would need his help and instead of enacting revenge upon them, he explained to them how he really saw things. He realized that God had ordered ALL his steps. He realized that this was what the Vision of reigning and ruling was all about. It was not to dictate over anyone but to save lives! Joseph told his brothers to not carry any guilt for what they had done to him because God used them to bring him to his Destiny! He told them to go tell his Father Jacob that he is alive and to bring him to him!

KINGDOM VISION is how Joseph was able to clearly see God's plan and not despise his own brothers as they had despised him. He gave them good for evil not because he was a human doormat for them to walk all over but because he lived and thought at a higher level that the love of God had taken him to. He had KINGDOM VISION that showed him he would win no matter what so that is why he was able to endure all the years of hardship, unfairness, betrayal and lies. It's amazing what you can go through when you already know you're going to make it! That is the power of what God can do for your life through a VISION OF VICTORY!

It comes down to us somewhat being able to see what God sees. That's how KINGDOM VISIONS OF VICTORY work. God does not see as man sees…God sees deeper. The Bible says that while "man sees the outward appearance; God sees the heart" **(1 Samuel 16:7)**. God has a probing way to see and dig out the goodness and potential of people and He longs to empower us to do the same. If we see life, then we'll speak life and Kingdom Living is all about speaking life! If we are to prepare the Kingdom of God on Earth to one day join the Kingdom of Heaven then we have to start functioning on Earth as in Heaven!

Nothing in Heaven is sick, dying, broke, busted, or disgusted. Nothing in Heaven is depressed or defeated. It really comes down to what do you choose to see &

speak and how do you choose to live? As a Christian, we are simply called to live at a higher level. Not from a place where we act snooty like a modern-day Pharisee but from a place that we long to encourage others to live at too all because of the glorious love of Christ!

We must see this way…think this way…reason from a powerful place of high level intensity because that is what God has called us to. We are not low-level thinkers…the Bible calls us THE ELECT OF GOD! He chose us to reign with Him forever…it's time to get ready!!

In **Ezekiel Ch. 37**, God gave the Prophet Ezekiel a Vision from a Valley and in that Valley was nothing but dried up bones of dead carcasses. Absolutely no life whatsoever. God asks can they live? Why would God ask a question like this in an environment like that? …because He has a VISION OF VICTORY! The same Vision then intensely shifts from a Valley of dead bones to an exceedingly great Army that has risen up full of life and fight!

You see, God saw it all along and wanted to show the Prophet. He wants to show you and I the same things. He wants us to see what He sees. He has a plan to proclaim some incredible things through our lives just as He did through the Prophets, Patriarchs and Apostles of the Bible. We just have to be willing to see. Are you willing to see what God wants to show you? Are you willing to let Victorious Vision override current circumstances that may seem bleak? Are you willing to speak life where death is? Are you ready to see past the petty and prioritize the powerful? KINGDOM VISIONS OF VICTORY will take you there…let's go!

PRAY: "*Lord, show me Your Glory in every way by revealing Destiny, Purpose and Power for my life and future through Visions of Victory so that I will always see and know that there is so much more for me than could ever be against me. In Jesus' Holy, Everlasting Name, Amen!*"

CONCLUSION

WELL, WE HAVE reached the end of this first book. I sincerely hope that you thoroughly enjoyed it and will hold it's truths close to your heart. There is a better way to live the Christian Life. It's not because anything has been added to God's Word, it's what is revealed from His Word! We are called to *"be separate from this world"* (2 Corinthians 6:17). It doesn't mean we don't mourn when the world mourns or hurt when the world hurts, but it does mean that we are different. We are to function differently and deeper. We are to see and reason higher because we do so from a higher place, and we do this to reach people and multiply the Kingdom.

My prayer is that you take the teachings from this book and apply it to your everyday life. That you begin to see where people are coming from and start to see the root cause of issues that may rise up. You counter it with patience, prayer and God-given words that help solve disagreements instead of prolonging them.

It is time to know who you are. The Church has suffered from an identity crisis for too Long caused by religion. It is time to reap the benefits of having a tangible relationship with the King of Kings and Lord of Lords. We are Joint-Heirs with Christ, we are the Elect of God, we are Children of the Most High God and we shall reign and rule with Him in Eternity, so it is time to walk in our Kingdom Identity and possess the Kingdom Vision He has enriched us to have and live our best life now and do all we can to shine His Light in the time we have left until He returns! I pray the Lord bless you and keep you and thanks again so much for your sacrifice of time in reading this book.

Serving Christ Forever,
Pastor Daniel Parker

About the Author

DANIEL PARKER HAS been Lead Pastor at Christian Fellowship Church (CFC) in Elm City, NC for 13 years. He is also the Worship Leader for his church's Praise Team FREEEDOM and has written all original songs for their first ever album titled "JESUS OVER ALL." Pastor Daniel has a passion to teach generations to walk in their Kingdom Purpose every single day of their life.

There is a better way to live, and it's found in Kingdom Living. This is his first book concerning Kingdom Teaching and he feels optimistic there will be more. Pastor Daniel teaches weekly "live" and online every week on Sundays at 10am & Wednesdays at 7pm. Tune in to these Kingdom Teachings each week on Facebook or YouTube under CFC Sandy Cross. On the Facebook page you can find download instructions for Apple & Android so you can access the CFC ShareFaith App. Instructions for the App are also on their website: cfcsandycross.com along with other great features.

Pastor Daniel lives in the Sandy Cross Community of Nashville, NC. He has been married for 19 years to his wife Tiffany and they have two sons, Zachary & Jackson, and grandson Brian along with the family pets Rico & Sassy (cats).

Visit CFC online every week or in person at 7814 S. NC 58 Elm City, NC